FIRST SCIENCE

Light

by Mari Schuh

Consultant:
Duane Quam, M.S. Physics
Chair, Minnesota State
Academic Science Standards
Writing Committee

BELLWETHER MEDIA • MINNEAPOLIS, MN

Note to Librarians, Teachers, and Parents:

Blastoff! Readers are carefully developed by literacy experts and combine standards-based content with developmentally-appropriate text.

Level 1 provides the most support through repetition of high-frequency words, light text, predictable sentence patterns, and strong visual support.

Level 2 offers early readers a bit more challenge through varied simple sentences, increased text load, and less repetition of high frequency words.

Level 3 advances early-fluent readers toward fluency through increased text and concept load, less reliance on visuals, longer sentences, and more literary language.

Level 4 builds reading stamina by providing more text per page, increased use of punctuation, greater variation in sentence patterns, and increasingly challenging vocabulary.

Level 5 encourages children to move from "learning to read" to "reading to learn" by providing even more text, varied writing styles, and less familiar topics.

Whichever book is right for your reader, Blastoff! Readers are the perfect books to build confidence and encourage a love of reading that will last a lifetime!

This edition first published in 2008 by Bellwether Media.

No part of this publication may be reproduced in whole or in part without written permission of the publisher. For information regarding permission, write to Bellwether Media Inc., Attention: Permissions Department, Post Office Box 1C, Minnetonka, MN 55345-9998.

Library of Congress Cataloging-in-Publication Data
Schuh, Mari C., 1975–
  Light / by Mari Schuh.
    p. cm. – (Blastoff! readers) (First science)
  Summary: "First Science explains introductory physical science concepts about light through real-world observation and simple scientific diagrams. Intended for students in grades three through six"–Provided by publisher.
  Includes bibliographical references and index.
  ISBN-13: 978-1-60014-097-6 (hardcover : alk. paper)
  ISBN-10: 1-60014-097-1 (hardcover : alk. paper)
  1. Light–Juvenile literature. I. Title.
  QC360.S38 2008
  535–dc22   2007010297

Contents

What Is Light?

Sunlight can wake you up in the morning. It peeks through your curtains, telling you a new day is here.

But light is much more than an alarm clock. It lets you see the world around you. It helps you work and play.

Light is a form of **energy**. Energy is what makes things move, grow, or change. For example, light helps plants grow. Most plants would die without light.

Most kinds of light also warm things up. Sunlight warms this rocky beach. A light bulb left on for a long time can get very hot.

Sources of Light

Light always comes from a **source**. Fire and light bulbs are both sources of light. The sun is the brightest and most important light source of all. It is such a bright source of light that it would damage your eyes if you looked directly at it. Never look directly at the sun.

fun fact

Light moves faster than any other known force or object in the universe. It moves much faster than sound. In a thunderstorm, you see lightning before you hear thunder even though they happen at the same time.

Light Rays

You rarely see it happening, but the light from a source moves through the air until it hits you and everything around you. Light moves in straight paths called **rays**.

Sometimes an object blocks the light's path.
Then a shadow forms on the other side of
the object. The shadow is the area light
does not reach. Trees, rocks, and buildings
all block light. Your body blocks light too.

Even Earth blocks light. Sunlight only shines on one half of Earth at a time. The other half is in a shadow.

Earth is always rotating. Every point on Earth moves through the shadow and the light every day.

Have you ever rested in the sunlight inside your house? You can do that because your windows don't block light. The clear glass in windows is **transparent**. This means light can move through it. Can you think of something else transparent?

! **fun fact**
Scientific studies show dogs only see shades of gray and some blues and yellows. Can you imagine not seeing all the colors?

Reflection

Light lets you see everything around you, from the tiniest bug to the biggest mountain. Light **reflects** off of objects and enters your eyes. Your eyes send a message to your brain. Your brain understands the message. Your brain tells you about the color, size, and shape of everything you see.

Light colors like white and yellow reflect more light than dark colors. Many skiers wear sunglasses because white snow reflects a lot of light.

You see your reflection when you look into a mirror. Light reflects off of you, into the mirror, and back into your eyes. The smooth surface of a mirror is good at reflecting light.

Look at the moon in the night sky. It doesn't make its own light. The moon reflects light from the sun.

The moon doesn't reflect enough light to let you read. You will have to use your flashlight!

Glossary

energy—the ability to do work or make things grow, move, or change

ray—a straight line of moving light

reflect—when rays of light hit an object and bounce back in another direction

source—something that gives off light

transparent—able to let light pass through

To Learn More

AT THE LIBRARY
Cooper, Christopher. *Light: From Sun to Bulbs*. Chicago, Ill.: Heinemann, 2004.

Cooper, Jason. *Light*. Vero Beach, Fla: Rourke, 2003.

Ring, Susan. *Light and Shadow*. Mankato, Minn.: Yellow Umbrella, 2003.

Stille, Darlene R. *Light*. Chanhassen, Minn.: Child's World, 2005.

Trumbauer, Lisa. *All About Light*. New York: Children's Press, 2004.

ON THE WEB
Learning more about light is as easy as 1, 2, 3.

1. Go to www.factsurfer.com

2. Enter "light" into search box.

3. Click the "Surf" button and you will see a list of related web sites.

With factsurfer.com, finding more information is just a click away.

Index

The images in this book are reproduced through the courtesy of: Juan Martinez, front cover; ANP, pp. 4-5; Jorg Jahn, p. 6; Mikhail Nekrasov, p. 7; Ian O'Leary/Getty Images, p. 8; Cesair, p. 10; Lane V. Erickson, p. 11; Cristi Matei, p. 12-13; Stuart O'Sullivan, pp. 14-15; spe, p. 16; Tim Hall/Getty Images, p. 17; Richard Price/Getty Images, p. 18; Richard Koek, Getty Images, p. 19; Gerry Ellis/Getty Images, p. 20; Christoph Wilhelm/Getty Images, p. 21.